Text
STYLES

HOW TO TELL A

Folktale

Carol Alexander

Crabtree Publishing Company

www.crabtreebooks.com

Text STYLES

Author: Carol Alexander

Coordinating editor: Reagan Miller

Publishing plan research and development:
Sean Charlebois, Reagan Miller
Crabtree Publishing Company

Editorial director: Kathy Middleton

Print coordinator: Katherine Berti

Production coordinator: Margaret Salter

Prepress technician: Samara Parent

Logo design: Samantha Crabtree

Product development: Victory Productions, Inc.

Content Editor: Janet Stone

Photo research: Tracy Vancelette

Front cover: Characters from the following folktales appear: Paul Bunyan, How Crow Brought the Daylight, Coyote Trickster, and How the Rhino Got His Skin.

Title page: Paul Bunyan lived in an enormous log cabin in the logging area of the Midwestern United States.

Photographs:

Corbis: Blue Lantern studios: cover (Paul Bunyan), 5 (bottom)

Corel: 26 (top)

Wikimedia Commons: cover (How the rhino got his skin by Rudyard Kipling; World Book Company: Indian Days of the Long Ago by Edward S. Curtis)

Shutterstock: All other images

Illustrations:

Barbara Bedell: 26 (paint palette)

Katherine Berti: title page (bird)

Bonna Rouse: 9 (pine tree)

Cataloguing in Publication data available at Library and Archives Canada.

Cataloging-in-Publication data available at Library of Congress.

Crabtree Publishing Company

www.crabtreebooks.com   1-800-387-7650

Printed in Canada/082011/MA20110714

Published in Canada
Crabtree Publishing
616 Welland Ave.
St. Catharines, Ontario
L2M 5V6

Published in the United States
Crabtree Publishing
PMB 59051
350 Fifth Avenue, 59th Floor
New York, New York 10118

Published in the United Kingdom
Crabtree Publishing
Maritime House
Basin Road North, Hove
BN41 1WR

Published in Australia
Crabtree Publishing
3 Charles Street
Coburg North
VIC 3058

Contents

What is a Folktale?

Folktales are among the oldest stories ever told. Some folktales are hundreds of years old. People have passed down these stories from generation to generation. Folktales do not have a single author. They were told and retold by "folks," or common people. A similar tale may appear in many different cultures. Names and places are changed, but the story is really the same.

Why did people tell folktales?

Long ago, people had many questions that were hard to answer. Folktales helped people make sense of the world around them. A folktale can explain how something came to be. For example, it might tell how mountains were formed or why the sun rises and sets.

Every folktale has a hero.

The **hero** can be a person or an animal. He or she accomplishes great deeds. The hero is often strong, intelligent, loyal, and determined. This **character** may have special powers. In folktales, we meet animals that can talk. We take giant steps with the tallest man in the world. Yet, these are not silly stories. Folktales have a purpose. They both entertain us and teach us important lessons about life.

Some folktales are called "tall tales."

The heroes of **tall tales** accomplish impossible deeds. Have you heard of Pecos Bill or Paul Bunyan? They are characters with superpowers. In one folktale, the giant lumberjack Paul Bunyan tames a wild river. Of course, this could not really happen. But we are still amazed by Bunyan's actions. He never gives up, no matter how hard the job.

The trickster tale is another kind of folktale.

A **trickster** is a clever and sly character who outsmarts everyone in the story. Tricksters may cause trouble for other characters. But often, they also solve problems or learn lessons. In one story, we will meet Crow. Crow is the hero of an Inuit tale from Canada. This clever bird finds a way to bring light to the world.

Folktales share many common ideas. The stories show what people believe about the world. In many ways, we are all alike. We want to be clever and brave. We want to solve problems. Folktales teach us all of these things. Most importantly, they are fun to read!

Paul Bunyan Tames the Whistling River

Paul Bunyan was the tallest man in the land. In fact, he was a giant. Of course, his pet ox was a giant, too. Paul and Babe the Blue Ox made quite a team. Together, they took on the toughest jobs. They worked at a logging camp near the Whistling River. Tall pine trees surrounded the camp.

That old Whistling River was a terror. It had a mind and spirit of its own. Yes, its blue waters sparkled brightly. But this was a dangerous river with fast-moving waters. The river rose up and whistled twice a day. Its screeching could be heard for miles around. The river splashed the loggers with its mighty waves. It broke up logs and flooded the logging camp. The lumberjacks got pretty tired of these tricks. They hollered at the river, "You leave off that foolishness right now!" The river didn't care one little bit. It licked and lapped at the muddy shore. This was no ordinary river. It played its magic tricks day in and day out.

One day, Paul was sitting on a hill. He was combing his beard with a pine tree. What do you think happened? That river rose right up over its banks. It dumped a lake full of water on Paul's head! Paul went on combing his beard. Then the river pulled its favorite trick again. Mud and turtles rained down on Paul's head. Paul got mad and stamped his foot. He sure was fired up.

"That's enough, you old river! I'll tame you, sure enough. You'll carry logs to the mill like I tell you to!"

The river stuck out its tongue at Paul. Then it went its merry way. "Ha ha," it chuckled.

Paul Bunyan never backed down. He was going to teach that Whistling River a lesson! He made a plan to hitch Babe to that river and straighten it out. He would take away some of the river's power and make it behave. First, they'd need a little help. With a few giant steps, Paul and Babe reached the North Pole. Paul set a trap for icy storms.

There were plenty of blizzards at the North Pole. Meanwhile, Babe and he played fetch in the freezing ocean. They had to stop because Babe splashed too much. The waves she made soaked the coast of Florida!

At last, they trapped some icy winter storms. Paul took his box of blizzards back to the logging camp. There he found his friend Ole, another logger. Ole was the kind of friend a logger could depend on. Paul asked Ole for help.

"I need the world's heaviest chain," Paul told Ole.

Ole scratched his head. "Now, Paul, why do you need such a heavy chain?" Ole liked to take things slowly. He never looked for extra work.

"I'm gonna catch that pesky river."

"Ah, I reckon so." Ole put down his pipe and started making the chain for Paul.

Paul set a blizzard on each side of the river. That pesky river froze solid in no time at all. But the problem was not solved yet. Paul had to straighten that river out. He hitched Babe to the thick chain. The Big Blue Ox would need to pull the river quite a distance to make it straight.

What a job! The frozen river did not want to move an inch. Babe pulled and pulled. Then Paul gave her a hand. Together, they yanked the river from its muddy bed. They pulled it across the prairie until it was perfectly straight. Some of the river split off into smaller streams.

Then Paul took his rusty old saw and split those streams into small lengths. He rolled them up and tied them with rope. What did he do with those little creeks? Why, he used them to float his logs across dry land.

The Whistling River was tamed at last. It stayed in its place and minded its manners. The loggers cheered for Paul and Babe. Ole said, "I made a good, solid chain, I guess. But you and Babe did the hard work."

"Aw shucks, it was nothing," Paul said. That night, he ate five barrels of corn. Babe ate a couple of haystacks. Then, tired out from their busy day, they fell fast asleep.

Big Characters in a Tall Tale

What helps readers to recognize folktale characters?
Here are some tips. They are usually "flat" characters. They are just what they seem to be. The heroes have qualities we can admire. These qualities are called traits. A trait is a part of a hero's personality that does not change. The heroes are honest, brave, strong, and often clever. Other characters in the folktale may be dishonest, lazy, weak, and foolish. These characters may not change much, either.

In this story, Paul Bunyan is the main character. He is a friend to all lumberjacks. In some ways, he is just like the other loggers. He works hard, talks like a workingman, and enjoys a good joke. On the other hand, Paul is huge--at least eighteen feet tall (5.5 meters). Paul is a folklore hero. He is really someone to look up to! He solves a big problem for the loggers.

The Whistling River is another character in the story. In some ways, it is like a person. The river has an important job to do. It carries logs downstream to the mill. Its waters are blue and sparkling. But the river has another side.

The Whistling River makes mischief for the lumberjacks. In some ways, the river is an enemy of the loggers. But Paul is stronger and smarter than the river. He knows what is right and what is wrong. In the end, it is Paul who teaches the river a lesson.

One day, Paul was sitting on a hill. He was combing his beard with a pine tree. What do you think happened? That river rose right up over its banks. It dumped a lake full of water on Paul's head! Paul went on combing his beard. Then the river pulled its favorite trick again. Mud and turtles rained down on Paul's head. Paul got mad and stamped his foot. He sure was fired up.

"That's enough, you old river! I'll tame you, sure enough."

The river stuck out its tongue at Paul. Then it went its merry way. "Ha ha," it chuckled.

 What else do you notice about Paul and the river? On a separate sheet of paper, make a chart like the one below. Fill in your copy of the chart with three details about each character.

Paul Bunyan
Detail 1: a giant lumberjack
Detail 2: takes on tough jobs
Detail 3: ?

The Whistling River
Detail 1: splashes the loggers for fun
Detail 2: does what it wants to do
Detail 3: ?

Exploring Other Characters

Paul's friend Ole works at the logging camp. He plays a role in the folktale, too. We do not learn very much about Ole in this tall tale. But you can figure out some things about him. Read the tall tale again. Look for details about Ole. Then answer these questions:

- **How is Ole like Paul? How is he different?**

- **What problem does Ole help solve? What exactly does he do?**

- **How does Ole feel about the work he did?**

- **Could the story have turned out as well without Ole's help?**

Describe Characters

Now that we have learned the common traits of folktale characters, it is time to create your hero. Will your character be a person, an animal, or a part of nature? What traits will your hero possess?

Now, think about other characters in your tale. Who will be the hero's enemy? Imagine a character that makes problems for others. This character will be very different from the hero.

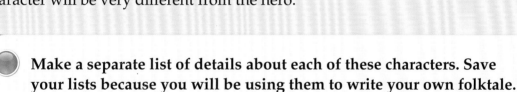

Make a separate list of details about each of these characters. Save your lists because you will be using them to write your own folktale. You can start your list like the one below and fill in the details:

- **This character is called**

  _____

- **The character looks/speaks/acts like**

  _____

- **He/she is good at**

  _____

- **He/she has a problem to solve/makes a problem for others. The problem is**

  _____

- **The hero can solve the problem because he/she is**

  _____

- **The enemy is overpowered because**

  _____

Dialogue and Dialect

 Dialogue **is common in folktales. The dialogue is what characters say to each other. The rest of the tale is told in the third person. This person is called the narrator. The narrator is outside of the story and is telling the tale.**

Dialogue brings characters to life. We can learn about what these people are thinking or feeling or doing from what they tell others. For example, here is what the loggers holler at the river:

 "You leave off that foolishness right now!"

We can tell the loggers are angry. The dialogue also shows how the loggers talk. The river can't "speak," of course. It answers by licking and lapping at the shore. The river laughs in the tall tale.

 Dialect is a form of speech used in a particular place or time. People may use grammar and words in a different way. We get an idea of how people spoke in that logging camp:

● *"I'm gonna catch that pesky river."*

● *"Aw shucks, it was nothing."*

Dialogue also moves the story forward:
"I need the world's heaviest chain."

"Now, Paul, why do you need such a heavy chain?"

"I'm gonna catch that pesky river."

"Ah, I reckon so."

● **What do you learn from this dialogue? How does Paul deal with problems? Why does he succeed?**

We can learn a lot about the characters from the way they speak. Paul is determined and will complete the task he sets out to do.

Dialect: It's All About How You Say It

Write down the dialogue in the folktale that includes dialect. Then write the dialogue in another way. Compare the words in the story to your own words. Does the meaning seem to change?

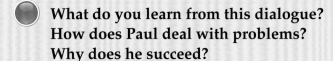

● **Add More Dialogue**
Think about ways to add more dialogue to this folktale. Find three places in the story where dialogue could work well. Add dialogue to show what a character is thinking or doing.

Setting: The Time and Place

The **setting** is where and when a story takes place. The setting of a folktale is usually simple. A few details about time and place set the scene. Our imaginations must fill in the rest of the setting. We do know that the story happened long ago. This is certainly true of "Paul Bunyan Tames the Whistling River." For example, Paul needs his ox to haul heavy things. There are no trucks or trains to haul logs.

The setting provides other clues, too. A river cannot stick out its tongue. It does not purposely soak people. We are in the land of make-believe.

 Which details from the passage tell you about the setting? Find other details about setting throughout the story.

 Paul Bunyan never backed down. He was going to teach that Whistling River a lesson!

First, they'd need a little help. With a few giant steps, Paul and Babe reached the North Pole. Paul set a trap for icy storms. There were plenty of blizzards at the North Pole. Meanwhile, Babe and he played fetch in the freezing ocean. They had to stop because Babe splashed too much. The waves she made soaked the coast of Florida!

 ## Write Your Own Setting
Think of a good setting for your own folktale. When and where will your folktale take place? List details about the setting of your folktale.

Plot: The Basic Outline

Every story has a **plot**. There is a beginning, middle, and ending. Events, or what happens in the folktale, make up the plot. The plot of a folktale is generally shorter and simpler than in other kinds of stories. The familiar story lines of folktales are exciting and fast paced.

We quickly learn that there is an important problem to be solved. Perhaps a mighty force of nature must be tamed. Sometimes, the hero fights an evil person. In some folktales, the main character must learn something about himself or herself. This problem tests the folktale hero. Another word for problem is **conflict**.

The **action** in the story gets more and more exciting. Then it reaches the **climax**, the most exciting part of the story. At last the problem is solved. That is the **resolution**, or solution. Folktales often have happy endings.

Think about the conflict in this folktale.

The Whistling River rises up twice a day. It dumps water on the logging camp. The river and the loggers become enemies. Paul Bunyan wants to teach the river a lesson. What happens next? Paul and Babe go to the North Pole. They catch some blizzards. They use the blizzards to freeze the river. Then Babe and Paul drag the frozen river over the prairie. The river is tamed. It cannot do any more harm.

A Good Problem for a Folktale

What problem will your story character solve? Write a paragraph about this conflict. Tell how the problem will be solved. Remember, you are in the land of make-believe. A folktale can have magic. Think of exciting ways to reach a solution.

Now you are ready to create a story map.

Story Map for "Paul Bunyan Tames the Whistling River"

Characters	Paul Bunyan, Babe, Ole, and the Whistling River
Setting	a logging camp near Whistling River
Problem	Whistling River makes trouble for the loggers.
Events	1. River soaks Paul Bunyan.
	2. Paul and Babe go to the North Pole to get blizzards.
	3. Paul and Babe haul the Whistling River over the prairie.
Resolution	The Whistling River is tamed.

Theme

A story's **theme** is its message or main idea. Folktales may share some common themes. For example, many tales teach that it is better to share than to be selfish. We may learn that patience wins in the end. Some stories show that hard work leads to satisfying results. Goodness is rewarded, and evil is punished. There are many themes. Which ones can you find in "Paul Bunyan Tames the Whistling River"? Read the text in the box to the right. What is the theme or message?

Paul Bunyan never backed down. He was going to straighten out that Whistling River.

What a job! The frozen river didn't want to move an inch. Babe pulled and pulled. Then Paul gave her a hand. Together, they yanked the river from its muddy bed. They pulled it across the prairie until it was perfectly straight.

A Personal Response

Now you know some important themes of this folktale. Think about the lessons the folktale teaches. Then write a paragraph about a lesson you learned from reading "Paul Bunyan Tames the Whistling River." Be sure to describe how particular events supported the theme.

Finding the Theme

The passage in the box above delivers a message, or theme. One of the themes is that we should never give up because hard work is the key to success. Working together is another theme in this folktale. Paul, Ole, and Babe all have an important job to do. We also learn that it is better to behave well than to behave badly.

Creative Responses to the Folktale

Tell All About It!

Imagine that you write for a newspaper. Write a newspaper story about the giant who tamed a wild river. Explain how Paul Bunyan used his wits to solve the problem. Let your readers know why Paul is a hero. Answer the questions Who? What? Where? Why? and How?

Using Words and Pictures

Draw a cartoon strip of the events in the folktale. Show the Whistling River, the log camp, Paul, Ole, and Babe the Blue Ox. Add words that describe what is in the picture boxes. Give your cartoon strip a title.

Write a Song

Write a song about Paul Bunyan and the Whistling River. Your song will help Paul and his deeds live on in history. Introduce listeners to this hero. Use descriptive words to tell the story. Make your song exciting to hear. If you like to compose music, add sound to your song.

Explaining Our World

Many folktales explain how our world works. The Inuit story "How Crow Brought the Daylight" does just that. The Inuit live in the frozen North in the Canadian Arctic. It is dark there for half the year. This is because the Arctic is tilted away from the sun during winter. In summer, the opposite happens resulting in six months of constant light.

Long ago, the Inuit told a different tale. They described how Crow brought them daylight. He flew to the sunny South. The clever bird managed to steal a ball of light. He journeyed back to the Inuit people. Now they too had light.

You will see that folktales have things in common. The tales can show how or why something happens. There are other ways that folktales are alike. The storytellers were telling these tales aloud. They did not read them or write them down. So they repeated certain words. We hear a lot about Crow "bringing the light." The words darkness, light, and daylight appear often. These words point to a main idea.

Each folktale has been told many times. Each teller changes the story just a bit. Some details are added or taken away. But the plot is always the same.

How Crow Brought the Daylight
--a folktale from the Inuit peoples of Arctic Canada

*L*ong ago, the Inuit people lived in darkness. The sun never shone in this land of ice and snow. People hunted in the dark. Their children played in the dark. They did not know any other life. One day, Crow flew back from a long journey.

"It is not always dark in the South," Crow told the people. "Each morning, the sky is filled with light."

The Inuit did not believe this story. How could it be true? Yet, they wanted to hear the story again. Over and over, Crow described the sunny lands. He told them about green trees and blue waters. He told them about yellow flowers. The world of light was very beautiful.

"Go back to that place," the Inuit leader said. "Bring us light. "

"Yes! We will be able to hunt better. Our children will play safely outside."

"No," Crow said. "I am getting old. I cannot make another journey south."

But the people begged Crow. "Please bring us light! Only you can do it."

"Very well," Crow said with a sigh. "I will do my best."

So off he flew. He came to the land of light. He saw rivers and trees. He saw beautiful mountains where wild flowers grew. The sun poured down like honey. It was almost too much!

Crow rested on a tree branch. The sparkling river rushed on. A girl came to the river with her bucket. She dipped the bucket into the river. Then she went off to her village.

Crow turned himself into a speck of dust. Nobody could see him now. He hid in the girl's scarf. She entered her home and brought the water to her son and the child's grandfather. This was the chief of the tribe. Crow knew he had come to the right place.

The clever bird settled in the little boy's ear. The child began to weep because of the speck of dust in his ear.

"Oh, what is wrong?" The chief hated to see his grandson cry.

Crow whispered, "You want to play with a ball of daylight."

The child spoke Crow's words aloud.

The chief nodded. The girl brought him the special box. In that box was a glowing ball. The chief tied a string to the ball of light. He placed the string in the boy's hand.

Crow knew what to do. He tickled the boy's ear. "You want to go outside and play."

The child repeated Crow's words. "Of course," the chief said. And the little family went out into the snow.

Then Crow took on his real shape. He snatched the string from the boy. Away he flew. He did not stop for many days. Finally, he reached the village in the dark North.

The Inuit came from their snow lodges. "We missed you!" they cried. They were so happy to see Crow again. What happened then? Crow dropped the ball on the ice. The ball smashed into tiny pieces. Up flew the daylight. A golden sun appeared in the sky. The icy land glittered. People covered their eyes. It was almost too much!

The children laughed and pointed at the sun. The mountains looked purple in the distance. There were soft, white clouds in the blue sky. Such beauty! Such wonder!

"But daylight will not last forever," Crow explained. "I could only bring back one ball of light. After six months, the ball must rest. Then it will be dark again. But the light will return."

"Ah," said the Inuit leader. "That is good. We have lived in darkness for so long. We can live in darkness for half the year."

That is how it happened. For six months each year, the Inuit have daylight. For the other six, their land is dark. Crow is their hero. After all, he brought them light.

Trickster Characters

A folktale hero—often an animal—can be a trickster. This animal behaves like a clever person. You might think that it is not nice to play tricks on people, but the trickster plays a special role. He or she wants to help others. The character solves a problem by playing a trick.

Crow is a friend to the Inuit. He finds a way to bring them daylight. He has to change shape to do this. That happens in some other trickster tales, too. Crow and Paul Bunyan have special powers. In other folktales, the hero may just be an ordinary person.

 What did you learn about Crow from this tale? Look at the word web.

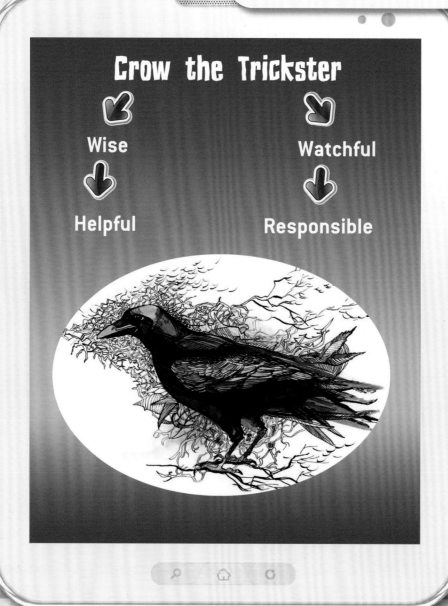

Crow the Trickster

Wise

Watchful

Helpful

Responsible

The words in the word web can all be used to describe Crow. Now, read these three passages from the folktale. Use the passages and other information from the folktale to complete the chart that follows.

But the people begged Crow. "Please bring us light! Only you can do it."

"Very well," Crow said with a sigh. "I will do my best."

Crow turned himself into a speck of dust. Nobody could see him now. He hid in the girl's scarf. She entered her home and brought the water to her son and the child's grandfather. This was the leader of the tribe. Crow knew he had come to the right place.

Then Crow took on his real shape. He snatched the string from the boy. Away he flew. He did not stop for many days. Finally, he reached the village in the dark North.

The Inuit came from their snow lodges. "We missed you!" they cried. They were so happy to see Crow again.

Who is Crow?	
What He Says	
What He Does	
What Others Say About Him	

Compare Two FolkTale Characters

You have read two folktales in this book. Think about Paul Bunyan and Crow. How are they alike? How are they different? How do these heroes go about solving problems? Discuss these questions with a partner.

Develop a Character

You have already thought about a character for your folktale. What else is important about this person or animal? Does he or she have special powers? Add to the list of details you began earlier.

Dialogue: Developing Characters

You have seen how writers use dialogue. Remember, dialogue has different purposes. It can show why something happens in the story. Here, Crow has just come back from the South.

Crow has just told the people of the village something they did not know. This information changes their view of the world.

"It is not always dark in the South," Crow told the people. "Each morning, the sky is filled with light."

Why are Crow's words important to the story? How do the Inuit people feel about his discovery? What happens after Crow speaks these words?

Dialogue also gives us information about story characters. When Crow speaks, he shows his age and experience.

"I am getting old. I cannot make another journey south."

"But daylight will not last forever," Crow explained. "I could only bring back one ball of light. After six months, the ball must rest. Then it will be dark again. But the light will return."

What do these speeches tell you about Crow? What has he learned from his experiences? Can you think of other wise story characters from movies or books?

Crow the Trickster uses language to fool the chief. Find Crow's whispered speeches to the chief's grandson. Why does Crow tell the child to do these things? How does the dialogue show the way Crow thinks? How do Crow's words move the plot forward?

Finding Your Voice
Imagine that you are a character in this story. Write a speech or a conversation you might have with another character. Be sure the speech you write fits in with and supports the meaning of this folktale.

Setting: A Long Time Ago

Setting is very important in "How Crow Brought the Daylight." We need to know when a story takes place. We know that this folktale comes from long ago. The Inuit have no sunlight. Here is another clue that the tale is set in the past: The Inuit do not know what life is like in other places. There are no radios to report the weather or the time of sunrise. There are no televisions or cameras to show the Inuit pictures of sunny lands.

Remember that setting also means where a story takes place. There are actually two settings in this story. There is the Inuit village of the North and an unnamed land of the South. Crow flies between these two lands. The tale includes a number of important details about each place. Read these descriptions of Inuit country:

- lived in darkness
- sun never shone
- snow lodges
- ice

Compare Two Settings

Which details describe the other setting in the story? Make a list of these details. Then copy the diagram below to record what is alike and different about the two settings in "How Crow Brought the Daylight." In the space on the left, write details that describe only the Inuit land. In the space on the right, write details that describe only the southern land Crow discovered. In the middle of the diagram, write details that describe both settings.

Inuit Land	Both	Southern Land

More About Plots

Let's look at plot again. As you already know, every story has a beginning, middle, and ending. The beginning of the story includes setting details. This is also where we meet the main character.

The writer quickly introduces a problem, or conflict. Perhaps the tribe must find an answer to a big question. Why does the sun rise? Where does the North Wind come from? Why are there four seasons?

The middle of the story tells what the main character does to fix the problem. More characters may come on the scene. The events lead to a climax. In a trickster folktale, the trick is usually the climax.

After the climax, the events lead to the resolution, or solution. The folktale must end well. A character makes a discovery or performs a great deed. He or she may learn an important lesson. Now the world makes more sense to people.

Story Map
A plot plan can help you outline your folktale.

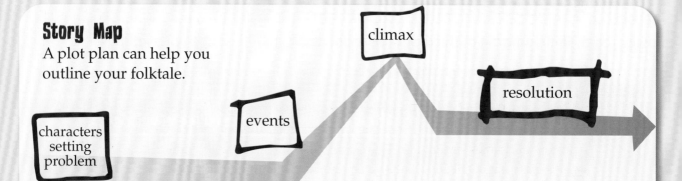

climax

events

resolution

characters
setting
problem

Using a Plot Plan
Copy this plot map on a large sheet of paper. That way, you will have plenty of room to write down the events. Put one or two events from "How Crow Brought the Daylight" in each part of the story map.

More About Theme

Folktales are a special kind of story. These tales are shared memories. They belong to a particular group of people. The stories live on because they are important in some way. A folktale may tell how a character helps others. A tale may explain something about the natural world, or about human nature.

The folktale hero faces special challenges. He or she must do what most others cannot. Paul Bunyan is a giant who moves a river. Crow is a trickster who outsmarts a wise chief to get a magic ball. These tales have a common theme.

Finding Common Themes

What exactly is the common theme? Think about the two folktales you have read. Answer the questions below.

- What is alike about the experiences of Paul Bunyan and Crow?

- How do others feel about these characters?

- What ideas in the stories seem to belong to an earlier time?

- What ideas in the stories still seem true today?

- What lesson does each folktale teach?

What did you find out as you answered these questions? Maybe you have already found some common themes. Here are a few examples of common themes to get you started: Heroes help others. There is a reason for everything in nature. It is good to take responsibility. Maybe you have found some other themes, too.

An Important Message

What will the theme of your folktale be? Will there be more than one theme? What message do you want to give your readers? Write down your ideas. You will be using them soon.

Creative Response to the Folktale

Do You See What I See?

Imagine that you are an Inuit child who watches as Crow brings the light to your village. Write a dialogue in which you and a neighbor share your feelings about the world you are seeing clearly for the first time. In your dialogue, describe this bright new world for your readers.

Perform It!

Act out the main scene from "How Crow Brought the Daylight." With a partner or group of classmates, show how Crow played his trick and carried off the ball of light. Actors can make up their own dialogue or use dialogue from the folktale.

Picturing the Action

Choose a part you liked best from "How Crow Brought the Daylight." Draw a picture of this scene, using details from the folktale. When you have finished your drawing, display it on the wall of your classroom.

Writing a Folktale

Prewriting

It is time for you to write your own folktale. What kind of folktale will you write? It could be a tall tale like "Paul Bunyan Tames the Whistling River." Maybe you will decide to write a trickster tale like "How Crow Brought the Daylight." Your story can take place in the past or the present. You can describe a real setting or a make-believe place.

1. Choose a Topic

You have already made some notes for your story. You have several ideas about the main characters and the problem to be solved. Now it is time to narrow down these ideas. Here are some points to think about:

- **Am I writing a tall tale or a trickster tale?**
- **What is the purpose of my tale?**
- **What can a reader learn from my folktale?**
- **Who will read my finished folktale?**

2. Explore Your Character

What will your main character be like? Look back at the notes you have made. Add more details to your notes. What does the character look like? How does he or she speak? What do others notice about this character? What does this character say about himself or herself?

3. Map it Out

Make a story map for your folktale. Look back at the two kinds of story maps in this book. Choose one of these for your own map. Make sure your map includes: a setting with details about the time and place; a main character, or hero; a problem the hero must solve; events; a climax; a resolution that wraps up the story.

4 Write a First Draft

Write your first draft. Do not stop to correct your mistakes. Just get your ideas down. Keep your story map handy as you write. It will help you to organize the events and details of your folktale. Keep these questions in mind:

● **How do I introduce the characters?**

● **How does each character look, speak, and act?**

● **Where can I use each character's exact words?**

Sandy is working on a trickster tale. She introduces a trickster character and sets out a problem for the trickster to solve. Below is the beginning of her first draft. Read the introduction of her folktale.

How Squirrel Fed Her Neighbors

Squirrel was busy all year. She ran up and down trees. In the forest. She was always having fun. All summer she visited her naybors. She made picnic baskets for everyone. There was plenty of food for all.

Then winter came. It was cold. There was snow. Squirrel got hungry. Were was all the food? Chipmunk said she was really hungry.

Squirrel said no. She had no basket. There was little to ear, there were no berries now.

She went to the Iak Tree. "Do you have any acorns?"

"No acorns for you," Oak Tree said. "I am saving them"

"I see," Squirrel answered.

"Stop bothering me." That is what Oak Tree told Squirrel.

Squirrel thought about things. Everyone was hungry. Squirrel knew she was clever. She hid acorns.

Revise Your Folktale

Read over your folktale. Add dialogue and description. Make sure the problem in your story is clear. Make these changes on a separate sheet of paper.

Sandy will make changes to the beginning of her folktale. She made her writing stronger. Think about what you will change in your folktale.

How Squirrel Fed Her Neighbors

Squirrel was busy all year. She ran up and down trees. In the forest. She was always having fun. All summer she visited her naybors. She made picnic baskets for everyone. There was plenty of food for all.

Then winter came. It was cold and snowy. Squirrel grew a warm, gray coat, But she got hungry. Were was all the food?

Chipmunk squeaked," Squirrel, we are hungry too. Do you have a picnic basket?" Poor Chipmunk was shivering in the cold.

Squirrel said no. She had no basket. There was little to eat because there were no berries now." "But I might have an idea," she said.

Squirrel went to Iak Tree. "Do you have any acorns?" "No acorns for you!" Oak Tree shouted". I am saving them." She waved her branched to scare Squirrel away.

" I see," Squirrel answered." Hm. That sounds a little selfish."

" stop bothering me." That is what Oak Tree told Squirrel." I need those little acorns. Theya re like my children. They will grown into tall trees like me.:

Squirrel thought about her neighbors. Everyone was hungry. Squirrel knew she was clever. She would figure out a plan.

"Ah ha!" she told herself". I think I have an idea." She dug into the snow and found a few acorns. Then she found a few more. She would hide them in her tree house!

Proofread Your Draft

Read your draft carefully. Did you spell all words correctly? Check words in a dictionary if you are unsure of the spelling. Does it have any run-on sentences or sentence fragments? Make corrections now.

Make a Final Copy

Now, copy your final draft on a separate sheet of paper. Share your folktale with your family and friends.

> Sandy proofread her trickster tale. She corrected sentence fragments and run-ons. She fixed errors in grammar, capitalization, and spelling.

How Squirrel Fed Her Neighbors

Squirrel was busy all year. She ran up and down trees in the forest. She was always having fun. All summer she visited her ~~naybers~~ neighbors. She made picnic baskets for everyone. There was plenty of food for all.

Then winter came. It was cold and snowy. Squirrel grew a warm, gray coat, But she got hungry. Where was all the food?

Chipmunk squeaked, "Squirrel, we are hungry too. Do you have a picnic basket?" Poor Chipmunk was shivering in the cold.

Squirrel said no. She had no basket. There was little to eat because there were no berries now. "But I might have an idea," she said.

Squirrel went to Oak Tree. "Do you have any acorns?" "No acorns for you!" Oak Tree shouted. "I am saving them." She waved her branches to scare Squirrel away.

"I see," Squirrel answered. "Hm. That sounds a little selfish."

"stop bothering me," Oak Tree told Squirrel. "I need those little acorns. They're like my children. They will grow into tall trees like me."

Squirrel thought about her neighbors. Everyone was hungry. Squirrel knew she was clever. She would figure out a plan.

"Ah ha!" she told herself. "I think I have an idea." She dug into the snow and found a few acorns. Then she found a few more. She would hide them in her tree house!

Glossary

action	All of the events in the story
character	Person or animal in a story
climax	Point of greatest excitement or tension
conflict	The problem to be solved in the tale
dialect	The way people of a particular region speak
dialogue	Exact words spoken by characters
folktale	A tale handed down from one generation to another
hero	Most important character in a folktale
plot	All of the action in the story
resolution	Part of the story that shows how the problem or conflict is solved
setting	Time and place in which a story unfolds
story map	A diagram that shows the basic parts of the plot
tall tale	Story with a "larger than life" hero who does great deeds
theme	Main idea or message of a tale
trickster	Folktale hero, usually an animal, who plays tricks to solve problems

Index

Further Resources

Books:

Coyote Rides the Sun: A Native American Folktale by Amanda St. John. Child's World, Inc. (2011)

Folktales on Stage: Children's Plays for Readers Theater by Aaron Shepard. Shepard Publications (2003)

Nelson Mandela's Favorite African Folktales by Nelson Mandela (Compiler). Hachette Audio; Unabridged edition (2009)

Raven: A Trickster Tale from the Pacific Northwest by Gerald Mcdermott. Houghton Mifflin Harcourt (2001)

The Classic Tales Of Brer Rabbit by Joel Chandler Harris. Running Press (2008)

Websites:

This site features folktales, fairy tales, and fables from around the world. http://worldoftales.com

This site introduces the folktale genre, as well as a variety of illustrated folktales from different cultures. www.pitara.com/talespin/folktales.asp

This site includes folktales from around the world as well as a writing workshop with real folktale writers! http://teacher.scholastic.com/writewit/mff/index.htm